Nelson Phonics
Spelling and Handwriting

Pupil Book

Red
2

Anita Warwick   Nicola York
Series Editor: John Jackman

OXFORD
UNIVERSITY PRESS

Great Clarendon Street, Oxford, OX2 6DP, United Kingdom

Oxford University Press is a department of the University of Oxford.
It furthers the University's objective of excellence in research, scholarship,
and education by publishing worldwide. Oxford is a registered trade mark of
Oxford University Press in the UK and in certain other countries

Text © Anita Warwick and Nicola York 2010
Series editor: John Jackman
Original illustrations © Oxford University Press 2014

First published by Nelson Thornes Ltd in 2010
This edition published by Oxford University Press in 2014

British Library Cataloguing in Publication Data
Data available

978-1-4085-0606-6

10 9 8 7 6

Printed in China by Leo Paper Products Ltd.

Acknowledgements

Cover photograph: Alan Rogers
Logo: John Haslam
Illustrations: Alan Rogers; Andy Peters; and Mike Philips at Beehive Illustrations
Page make-up: Wearset Ltd

The authors and publishers wish to thank the following for permission to use
copyright material:

Born on page 5: newborn baby boy © iStockphoto. **Sort** on page 5: child at school
© Laurence Mouton/www.photolibrary.com. **Fort** on page 12: Peter Scholey/
www.photolibrary.com; aerial view. **Toad** on page 13: natterjack toad (bufo
calamita) adult, crawling on moss, Sussex, England © Derek Middleton/FLPA.
Town on page 14: Wareham town and quay, River Frome, Dorset, England @ Jinny
Goodman/Alamy. **Cow** on page 14: © Fogstock/www.photolibrary.com. **Clown**
on page 15: street performer dressed as a clown at the Edinburgh Fringe Festival
2009 © Guillem Lopez/Alamy. **Frown** on page 15: Radio and television presenter
John Humphrys outside BBC Broadcasting House in London © Tim Graham/Alamy.
Toil on page 17: morning shot of garden nursery workers @ iStockphoto.

Although we have made every effort to trace and contact all copyright holders
before publication this has not been possible in all cases. If notified, the publisher
will rectify any errors or omissions at the earliest opportunity.

Links to third party websites are provided by Oxford in good faith and for
information only. Oxford disclaims any responsibility for the materials contained
in any third party website referenced in this work.

Contents

Can a horse run in shorts?

Copy the letters into your book.

or *or or or or*

sat

Copy and finish the words.

word bank

for   thorn
fork   torn
cork   worn
fort   cornet
short horse
sort   stork
cord   shorts
corn   he
born

 sh___ts

 h___se

f__k

c___n

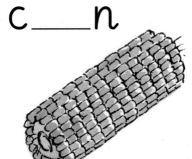

c___net

Find six **or** words in the grid.
Write the words.

a	d	v	q	q	j	c	b
c	x	s	c	p	g	m	or
z	e	or	d	x	h	j	n
f	or	t	t	c	i	m	l
b	p	u	c	or	n	k	w
t	r	z	k	n	g	f	v
w	or	n	l	e	sh	or	t
u	e	k	v	t	y	x	h

TIP Remember to join the letters **o** and **r**.

Copy the correct spelling for each word.

stork / stawk

thorn / torn

chort / short

5

Park the car in the farmyard.

Focus A

Copy the letters into your book.

Focus B

Copy and finish the words.

w o r d b a n k

arm	cart
bar	card
car	hard
jar	yard
bark	shark
park	harp
sharp	market
arch	farmyard
march	she

___ch

j___

p___k

c___d

c___

Red 18: To hear and say the /ar/ phoneme; to recognise and join the letters 'ar'.

Copy the words which do not rhyme.

hard   yard   jar

park   bark   market

sharp   cart   harp

arch   bar   march

Look at the picture. Say the word.
Use your fingers to count and say the sounds.
Now write the word.

TIP Remember to join the letters **a** and **r** using a diagonal joining line.

_____

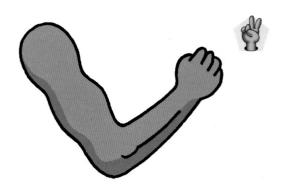

_____

_____

Is that a curl in his fur?

Focus A

Copy the letters into your book.

ur

Focus B

w o r d b a n k

fur	surf
burn	turf
urn	turn
burp	turnip
curl	we
hurl	
hurt	

Copy and finish the words.

s___f

b___n

c___l

f___

t___nip

Find the right word.
Copy and complete the sentences.

The sharp stick might _____ me.   (hurt **or** burn)

My dad has a big _____ in his garden.   (turnip **or** turn)

Sam wants to _____ in the sea.   (fur **or** surf)

Extension

Create and write your own words.

h		urn		
ch		orn		
b	**+**	arp	**=**	**?**
sh		urt		
c		ark		
th		ord		

Betty Batter had better butter.

Focus A

Copy the letters into your book.

er   .↗   er   .   er   .   er   .   er

Focus B

Can you spot the double letters before **er**?
Copy and finish the words.

word bank

better hammer
butter summer
letter locker
banner rocker
runner boxer
dinner cooler
hotter water
ladder me
supper

 lett___

lock___

 rock___

 hamm___

dinn___

runn___

Copy and complete the sentences.

What is it?

It is a _____. ladder **or** lader?

It is _____. supper **or** super?

It is a _____. boxer **or** boxur?

Copy and complete a sentence that goes with the picture.

It is ___er in the ___er.

Match the rhyming words and write them.

surf		beep
sheep		spoon
sight		jar
coat		turf
moon		flight
rocker		short
fort		locker
car		boat

Extra

Copy the correct spelling into your book.

tood / toad

sant / sand

truck / truk

bell / bel

hook / hooc

shep / sheep

Extension

Write the whole words in your book.

to + night =

tur + nip =

mar + ket =

hair + net =

chi + cken =

How now, brown cow?

Focus A

Copy the letters into your book.

ow   ow   ow   ow

Focus B

Copy and finish the words.

t__n

word bank

now	down
cow	town
how	gown
row	brown
wow	frown
bow	clown
owl	are
howl	
towel	

c___

__l

t__el

d___n

Find six **ow** words in the grid.
Write the words.

b	k	q	v		w	a	a
t	e		f	h	ow		j
n	ow		y		t	d	ur
	ur	x		f		v	q
u			er	r	h		h
c	t	c	l	ow	n		ow
s	g	i		n		ur	l
a	u	p	v	m	d	c	t

TIP Remember to join the letters **o** and **w**.

Read the words below. Write two lists, one of real words and one of made-up words.

bow

lown

gown

brown

dow

nowel

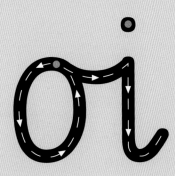

Find a coin in the soil.

Focus A

Copy the letters into your book.

Focus B

Copy and finish the words.

word
bank

oil	point
boil	noise
coil	poison
soil	cuboid
toil	noisy
coin	avoid
join	you
foil	
joint	

b___l

c___n

s___l

c___l

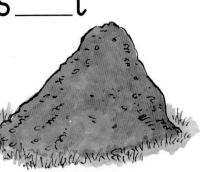

p___son

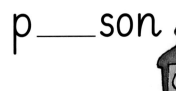

Write your own **oi** words.

 oi

TIP Remember to join the letters **o** and **i**.

Copy and complete the sentence with words containing **oi**.

We need to ___ in the ___.

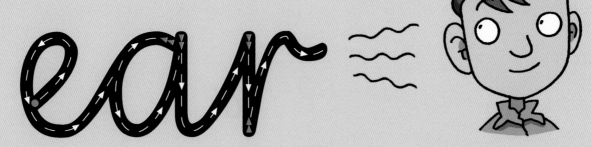

ear

You hear with your ear.

Focus A

Copy the letters into your book.

ear

Focus B

Copy and finish the words.

word bank

ear	tear
dear	year
fear	appear
gear	rear
hear	beard
near	they

t_____

app_____

f_____

g_____

r_____

Red 24: To hear and say the /ear/ phoneme; to recognise and join the letters 'ear'.

Use your fingers to count and say the sounds. Write the words.
Copy and complete a sentence to describe the picture.

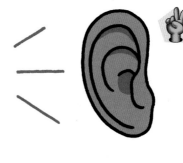

_____

_____

_____

b

ear

h

d

Copy and complete the sentence that goes with the picture.

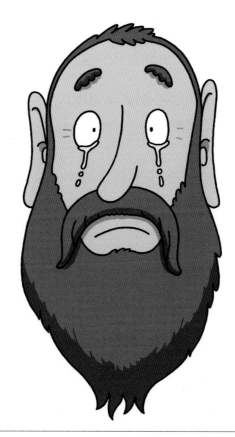

The man has _____.

TIP Remember to use a diagonal joining line to join these letters.

Put the chair upstairs.

Focus A

Copy the letters into your book.

air   *air   air   air*

Focus B

Make these **air** words.

word bank

air
fair
hair
pair
lair
chair
stair
upstairs
downstairs
my

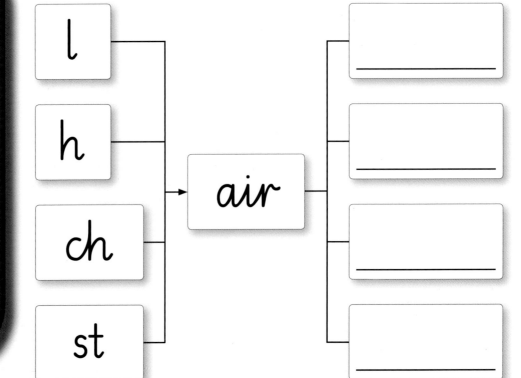

l

h

ch

st

→ air

Red 25: To hear and say the /air/ phoneme; to recognise and join the letters 'air'.

Find the right word.
Copy and complete the sentences.

We need _____ in our lungs. (air **or** hair)

He has a _____ of socks. (pair **or** pear)

Sam went to the _____. (fair **or** fur)

Copy and complete the sentence that goes with the picture.

The dragon had ten steps to his _____.

TIP Joining **r** to **e** is a tricky join – take care!

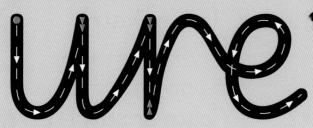

Is the vet sure of the cure?

Focus A

Copy the letters into your book.

ure *ure* *ure*

Focus B

Make these **ure** words.

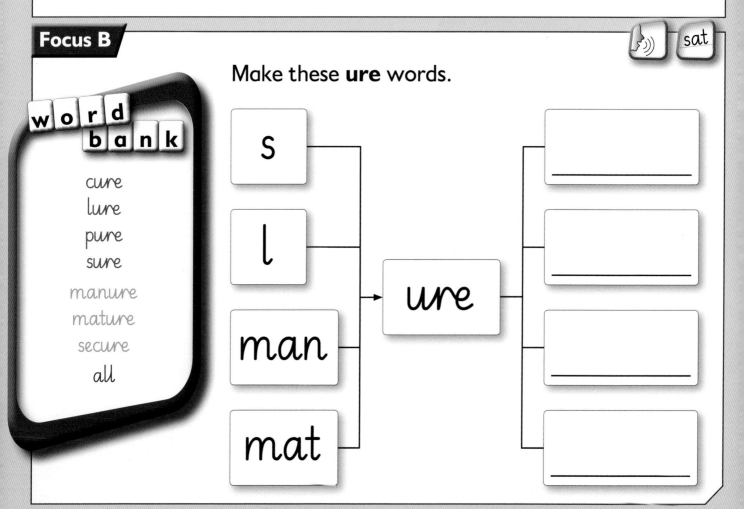

word bank

cure
lure
pure
sure
manure
mature
secure
all

s

l

man

mat

→ ure

Arrange the letters to spell each word correctly. Write the words.

crue

sercue

Extension sat

Write a sentence to go with the picture.

The vet has a ＿＿＿ for the dog.

Match the rhyming words and copy them.

cure

coin

clown

chair

hear

cow

soil

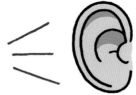

hair

boil

pure

now

down

join

dear

Copy the correct spelling for each word.

| towl / towel | stairs / stiars | cown / coin |

| goon / gown | secure / secyer | beard / beerd |

Read the word in each balloon.
Write the opposite word in your book.

soft

thin

long

far

blunt

nd
nt

Wind sent the tent into the pond.

Focus A

Copy the letters into your book.

nd   nt

Focus B

Copy and complete the words.

word bank

ant	rent	fond
pant	sent	pond
band	tent	wind
hand	went	mint
land	bend	was
sand	lend	
bent	mend	
dent		

a ____

wi ____

te ____

ha ____

mi ____

po ____

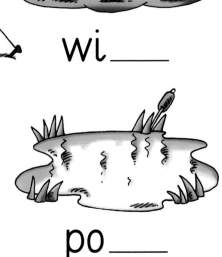

Read the words in each box. Copy the word which does not rhyme.

| tent   dent   mint |

| fond   pond   sand |

| band   land   bend |

| ant   pant   land |

Write the whole word.

| hu | + | nt | = | se | + | nt | =

| ha | + | nd | =

| re | + | nt | = | we | + | nt | =

| ba | + | nd | =

| me | + | nd | = | be | + | nd | =

br pr gr

Gran grabbed the green brush.

Focus A

Copy the letters into your book.

br   br   br   br   br   br   br   br

pr   pr   pr   pr   gr   gr   gr   gr

Focus B

 **word bank**

brim	grab
brick	gran
brush	green
brand	groan
brag	grow
pram	growl
print	be
prod	
prop	

Choose the correct blends.
Copy and complete these words.

___ush

___ick

___een

___an

___od

___am

Blend the two parts of the word together.
Write the word.

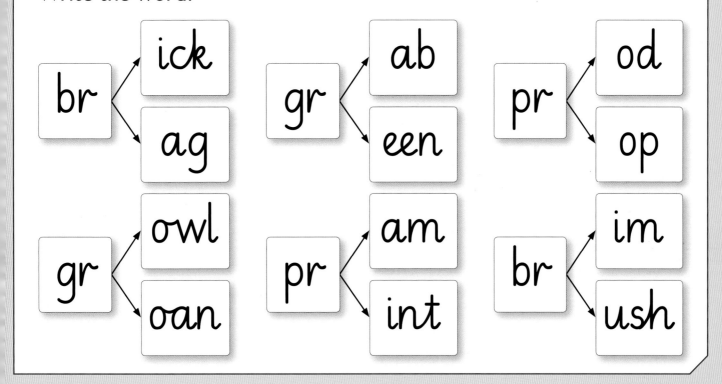

br → ick / ag

gr → ab / een

pr → od / op

gr → owl / oan

pr → am / int

br → im / ush

Write your own words beginning with **br**, **gr** or **pr**.
Use your fingers to say and count the sounds.

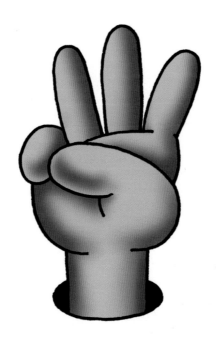

Tricky words

TIP Remember the letter **e** starts near the bottom, close to the line.

They said he has her red head band.

Focus A

Practise joining to and from the letter **e**.

ey   *ey*   *ey*   *ey*   *ey*   *ey*   *ey*   *ey*

er   *er*   *er*   *er*   *he*   *he*   *he*   *he*

Focus B

Copy the correct spelling. Put a dot or line under each sound, for example, wａṣ, a̲r̲e̲, yọu̲.

was / woz	are / ar
you / yoo	my / migh
they / thay	hur / her
orl / all	be / bee

Copy and complete each sentence using a tricky word.

my
she
be
are
all
you
was
her

_____ can come to play.

That is _____ cat.

I want to _____ a vet.

We _____ in the park.

It _____ hot in Spain.

Can _____ see the film?

_____ dress is green.

We can _____ swim in the sea.

Making sentences

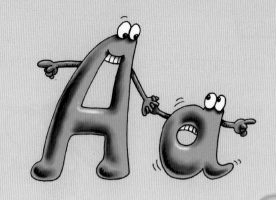

TIP Remember capital letters are used at the start of a sentence!

Focus A

Copy the capitals and the small letters.

Aa Aa Bb Bb Cc Cc Dd Dd Ee Ee Ff Ff

Gg Gg Hh Hh Ii Ii Jj Jj Kk Kk Ll Ll Mm Mm

Nn Nn Oo Oo Pp Pp Qq Qq Rr Rr Ss Ss Tt Tt

Uu Uu Vv Vv Ww Ww Xx Xx Yy Yy Zz Zz

Focus B

sat

Write these sentences with capital letters and full stops.

this clock has a beard

the boy is in the hole

my dinner is in the bath

his rat is on my bed